WALKING BASS LINE CONSTRUCTION
F BLUES

from the *Pathways Towards Greatness* series

by Bob Sinicrope

SHER MUSIC CO.

© 2024 Sher Music Co., P.O. Box 445, Petaluma, CA, 94953 All Rights Reserved.
International Copyright Secured. Made in the U.S.A. No part of this book may be reproduced
in any form without written permission from the publisher.
ISBN –978-0-9910773-3-5

TABLE OF CONTENTS

About *Walking Bass Line Construction - F Blues and Pathways Towards Greatness* series......iii

About the Author iv

Acknowledgements v

Online Hyperlinks Library vi

Chapter 1 Roots - Internalizing Roots 1

Chapter 2 Add the 5th - Internalizing Roots & 5ths 14

Chapter 3 Add the 3rd - Internalizing Root & 3rds 24

Chapter 4 Add the 7th - Internalizing Seventh Chords 32

Chapter 5 One Measure Patterns 37

Chapter 6 More Patterns 46

Chapter 7 Bass Lines in the Style of 51

          Pops Foster and Walter Page 52

          Milt Hinton and Slam Stewart 53

          Jimmie Blanton and Israel Crosby 54

          George Duvivier and Oscar Pettiford 55

          Percy Heath and Sam Jones 56

          Ray Brown and Red Mitchell 57

          Leroy Vinegar and Andy Simpkins 58

          Paul Chambers and Ron Carter 59

          Charlie Haden and Miroslav Vitous 60

          Bass Line from Backing Track 61

ABOUT WALKING BASS LINE CONSTRUCTION - F BLUES AND THE PATHWAYS TOWARDS GREATNESS SERIES

Walking Bass Line Construction — F Blues

This book is dedicated to helping you develop walking bass lines. It is designed for those with potentially limited knowledge of how to spell chords and/or have limited experience with a bass, but advanced players will find it useful as well. Most of the exercises in this book have a limited range - low E to middle C on the staff. For 4 string traditional tuning electric bass players this means all the exercises stay within the first five frets. The option to have tablature will be very beneficial to electric bass players.

By no means is this method complete, but it is an efficient way to create bass lines without a mastery of playing or theory. Playing these exercises correctly is a start. Internalizing and integrating these bass lines so you can apply them to other tunes is the goal. Strive to understand the underlying concepts of each exercise. Make them part of your musical vocabulary.

As useful as these exercises might be, the best way to learn bass lines is to emulate aspects of masterful bass lines you hear on recordings. Have fun and play with confidence and joy.

This book is part of the **Pathways towards Greatness** series. Other **Walking Bass Line Construction** books in the works include *All the Things You Are, Autumn Leaves, Bb Blues, Bb Rhythm Changes, C minor Blues, Perdido, Satin Doll, So What, Summertime, Sugar* and *Take the A Train*.

ABOUT THE AUTHOR

photo by Jamey Aebersold

Bob Sinicrope is a consummate educator. He founded the Milton Academy Jazz Program in 1974 and directed it for 50 years. Winner of several national and international awards, the program produced many fine professional musicians, most notably Aaron Goldberg and Steve Lehman. His students performed at multiple Jazz Education conferences, twice at the White House, the North Sea, Fribourg, Viennes, and Montreux Jazz Festivals. They have performed for Eric Alexander, Jim Hall, Dave Holland, Abdullah Ibrahim, Elvin Jones, Steven King, Poncho Sanchez, James Taylor, Desmond Tutu, Kenny Werner, and Victor Wooten and Bass Extremes. Bob's other teaching credits include Jamey Aebersold's Summer Jazz Workshops (40 years), JazzWise Summer School (London, 12 years), and Victor Wooten's Berklee Bass Workshops (7 years). Although Bob has a master's degree in math education, his studies at Berklee College and private lessons with Charlie Banacos, Hal Galper, Rufus Reid, Bob Gullotti, and Mick Goodrick greatly helped him transition to becoming a full-time jazz educator.

In 2007, Bob became the inaugural recipient of the *John LaPorta - Jazz Educator of the Year*. He was a Trustee of the Jazz Education Network (JEN) and was JEN's elected President from 2014-2016. In 2010 Bob received the National Youth Development Council award for his service and also received DownBeat magazine's Jazz Education Achievement Award. Bob has authored several published magazine articles and wrote a chapter in South African bassist Johnny Dyani's biography *Mbizo-Johnny Dyani*. His **Pathways Towards Greatness** SmartMusic improvisation books are used in 61 countries and his series of **Walking Bass Line Construction** books are published by Sher Music.

Bob has made his mark internationally over the past six decades with clinics in schools and conferences on six continents. In 1972, Bob was commissioned to compose *A Question of Balance* for Jamaica's National Dance Theater Company. Since 1991 his special connections with South Africa began when Abdullah Ibrahim visited Milton Academy and invited the school's combo to tour South Africa. His Milton Academy student groups have toured South Africa more than a dozen times and Bob has taught and performed there many times without his students including directing a weeklong workshop for over 100 students at Tshwane University in Pretoria. He also spearheaded the delivery of hundreds of thousands of dollars of donated materials and resources and has forged special bonds with many South African township music programs.

A much-in-demand bassist, Bob's credits include performances with Shirley Bassey, Jerry Bergonzi, Randy Brecker, Sara Caswell, John Clayton, Jeff Coffin, Billy Eckstine,

Bill Evans (saxophone), George Garzone, Aaron Goldberg, Tiny Grimes, Abdullah Ibrahim, Papa Jo Jones, Sean Jones, Mississippi Fred McDowell, Babatunde Olatunji, the Boston Pops, Chris Potter, Rufus Reid, Bobby Sanabria, Kenny Werner, Matt Wilson, Victor Wooten, and the Artie Shaw Band.

Bob can be reached by email at: bob.sinicrope@gmail.com
You can visit his website at: www.bobsinicrope.com

ACKNOWLEDGEMENTS

This method represents the current state of my ongoing learning and understanding of how to help students deepen their ability to freely express themselves in the jazz language. I have been very blessed to have learned from Jamey Aebersold, Christopher Azzara, David Baker, Charlie Banacos, Jerry Bergonzi, Steve Bailey, Gary Burton, Jerry Coker, Hal Crook, Hal Galper, Mick Goodrick, Edwin E. Gordon Bob Gullotti, Dan Haerle, John LaPorta, Harry Pickens, Herb Pomeroy, Rufus Reid, Kenny Werner and Victor Wooten. These wonderful players/teachers/learners have had a powerful impact on me. Being on the staff of the Aebersold Summer Jazz Workshops for over 40 years, and more recently the Victor Wooten Berklee Bass Weekend Workshop, has provided invaluable enrichment and inspiration.

This project has been greatly enhanced by my editor Eric Goode. His advice, keen eyes, perseverance, and encouragement were instrumental in getting this project to completion. John Goldsby was also very helpful with his wisdom, reading and editing. My appreciation also goes to Ted Scalzo for suggesting I share my teachings publicly and for his friendship.

A shout-out also goes to the fine musicians and technicians Mike DiLiddo (guitar and recording), Bobby Floyd (Hammond B3), Barry Lit (drums and recording), Austin Nill (recording), Joel Scanlon (mixing), and Ron Zack (piano) who recorded and/or produced the backing tracks. It was a pleasure for me to play bass with them on these tracks.

My heartfelt thanks goes to Chuck Sher for his encouragement, significant input, patience and long-standing friendship. It is an honor to be published by Sher Music given their ongoing commitment to jazz education.

Finally, and most significantly, my wife Frances Scanlon has been amazingly helpful with her gifted graphic design skills and editing, and more importantly, her love and support throughout. I thank her for her enthusiasm and commitment to me and this project.

ONLINE HYPERLINKS LIBRARY

This QR code will take you to an **online source of hyperlinks** to various sites that will deepen your understanding of some of the musical concepts presented in **Walking Bass Line Construction – F Blues**.

Each page of exercises has commentary and a title in *underlined text*.

This *underlined text* is an indication that the online source of hyperlinks can help you further your development.

CHAPTER 1

Roots - Internalizing Roots

F Blues
Walking Bass Line

Roots - Lower Chromatic to Root

Approach Notes are tension notes that resolve to chord tones. They add melodic interest and create rhythmic motion. The resolution is stronger if the approach note is on an upbeat and the chord tone is on a downbeat.

This exercise features **Lower Chromatic (LC)** approach notes to the **Root (R)**. These work well in bass lines.

Make it dance!

To more fully internalize:
1. *Listen*
2. *Sing*
3. *Play*

by Bob Sinicrope

Inspiration, Education, Fun
©2020 SeekingSpirit

Approach Notes are tension notes that resolve to chord tones. They add melodic interest and create rhythmic motion. The resolution is stronger if the Approach Note is on an upbeat and the chord tone is on a downbeat.

This exercise features **Lower Double Chromatic (LD)** Approach Notes to the **Root (R)**. These work well in bass lines.

Play with spirit!

F Blues
Walking Bass Line
Roots - Lower Double Chromatic to Root

To more fully internalize:
1. Listen
2. Sing
3. Play

by Bob Sinicrope

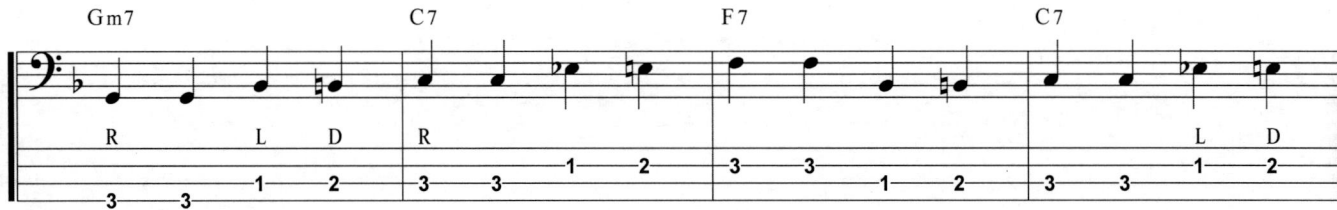

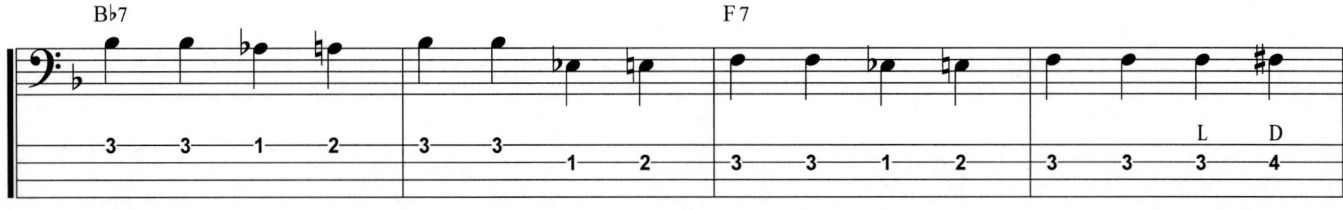

Inspiration, Education, Fun
©2020 SeekingSpirit

F Blues
Walking Bass Line
Roots - Lower Triple Chromatic to Root

Approach Notes are tension notes that resolve to chord tones. They add melodic interest and create rhythmic motion. The resolution is stronger if the Approach Note is on an upbeat and the chord tone is on a downbeat.

This exercise features **Lower Triple Chromatic (LTC)** Approach Notes to the **Root (R)**. These work well in bass lines.

Play with conviction!

To more fully internalize:
1. Listen
2. Sing
3. Play

by Bob Sinicrope

Inspiration, Education, Fun
©2020 SeekingSpirit

F Blues
Walking Bass Line
Roots - Upper Chromatic to Root

Approach Notes are tension notes that resolve to chord tones. They add melodic interest and create rhythmic motion. The resolution is stronger if the approach note is on an upbeat and the chord tone is on a downbeat.

This exercise features **Upper Chromatic (UC)** approach notes to the **Root (R)**. These do not always work well. Once you learn them, you can choose when you want to use them.

To more fully internalize:
1. Listen
2. Sing
3. Play

by Bob Sinicrope

Play with power!

Inspiration, Education, Fun
©2020 SeekingSpirit

WALKING BASS LINE CONSTRUCTION | F BLUES

F Blues
Walking Bass Line
Roots - Upper Double Chromatic to Root

Approach Notes are tension notes that resolve to chord tones. They add melodic interest and create rhythmic motion. The resolution is stronger if the Approach Note is on an upbeat and the chord tone is on a downbeat.

This exercise features a **Double Chromatic (UD) Approach Notes** to the **Root (R)**. These sometimes, but not always work well in bass lines.

Play with zest!

To more fully internalize:
1. Listen
2. Sing
3. Play

by Bob Sinicrope

Inspiration, Education, Fun
©2020 SeekingSpirit

WALKING BASS LINE CONSTRUCTION | F BLUES

F Blues
Walking Bass Line
Roots - Upper Triple Chromatic to Root

Approach Notes are tension notes that resolve to chord tones. They add melodic interest and create rhythmic motion. The resolution is stronger if the Approach Note is on an upbeat and the chord tone is on a downbeat.

This exercise features **Upper Triple Chromatic (UTC)** approach notes to the **Root (R)**. These do not always work well. Once you learn them, you can choose when you want to use them.

Make your notes ring out!

To more fully internalize:
1. *Listen*
2. *Sing*
3. *Play*

by Bob Sinicrope

Inspiration, Education, Fun
©2020 SeekingSpirit

F Blues
Walking Bass Line

Roots - Enclosure #3
Lower Double Chromatic - Upper Scalar to Root
Upper Scalar - Lower Double Chromatic to Root

by Bob Sinicrope

Enclosures combine Lower and Upper Approach Notes that resolve to chord tones. They add melodic interest and create rhythmic motion.

This exercise features **Lower Double Chromatics (LD)** and **Upper Scalar (US)** approach notes.

It also has **Forward Motion** where the approach notes resolve to a chord tone on a strong downbeat.

Play with expression!

To more fully internalize:
1. Listen
2. Sing
3. Play

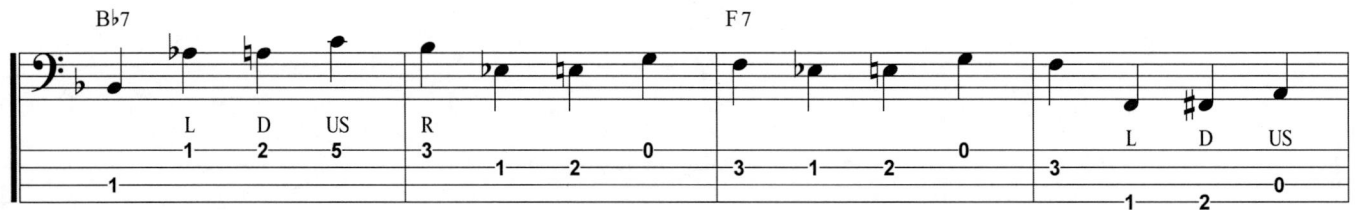

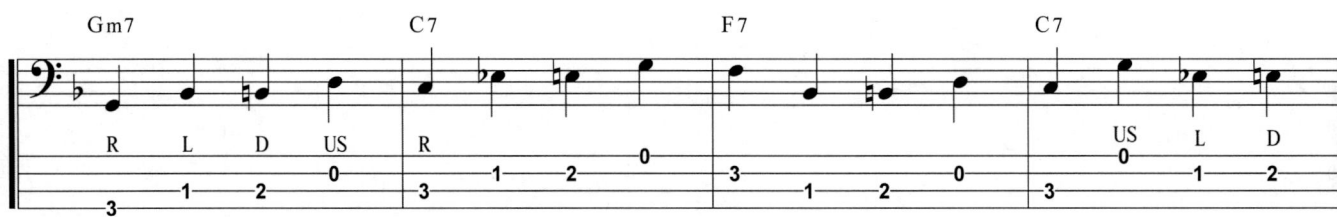

Inspiration, Education, Fun
©2020 SeekingSpirit

CHAPTER 2

Add the 5th - Internalizing Roots & 5ths

Bassists frequently utilize **Roots**, **5ths** and **Octaves** in their bass lines. These make a strong harmonic foundation. It's important to become comfortable with these patterns.

Sing and play **Roots (R), 5ths (5)** and **Octaves (R̂)** on all tunes to help internalize their sound.

Play with energy!

F Blues
Walking Bass Line
Add the 5th - Internalizing Roots & 5ths

To more fully internalize:
1. Listen
2. Sing
3. Play

by Bob Sinicrope

Inspiration, Education, Fun
©2020 SeekingSpirit

F Blues
Walking Bass Line
Add the 5th - Lower Chromatic to Root

Approach Notes are tension notes that resolve to chord tones. They add melodic interest and create rhythmic motion. The resolution is stronger if the approach note is on an upbeat and the chord tone is on a downbeat.

This exercise features **Lower Chromatic (LC)** approach notes to the **Root (R)** or **Octave (R̂)**. These work well in bass lines.

Tell a story when you play!

To more fully internalize:
1. Listen
2. Sing
3. Play

by Bob Sinicrope

Inspiration, Education, Fun
©2020 SeekingSpirit

18   WALKING BASS LINE CONSTRUCTION | F BLUES

Approach Notes *are tension notes that resolve to chord tones. They add melodic interest and create rhythmic motion. The resolution is stronger if the approach note is on an upbeat and the chord tone is on a downbeat.*

This exercise features **Upper Scalar (US)** *approach notes to the* **Root (R)** *and* **Octave (R̂)**.

Feel the pulse!

F Blues
Walking Bass Line
Add the 5th - Upper Scalar to Root

To more fully internalize:
1. *Listen*
2. *Sing*
3. *Play*

by Bob Sinicrope

Inspiration, Education, Fun
©2020 SeekingSpirit

F Blues
Walking Bass Line
Add the 5th - Lower Chromatic to 5th

Approach Notes *are tension notes that resolve to chord tones. They add melodic interest and create rhythmic motion. The resolution is stronger if the approach note is on an upbeat and the chord tone is on a downbeat.*

This exercise features **Lower Chromatic (LC)** approach notes to the **5th (5)**. These work well in bass lines.

Play with a beautiful sound!

To more fully internalize:
1. Listen
2. Sing
3. Play

by Bob Sinicrope

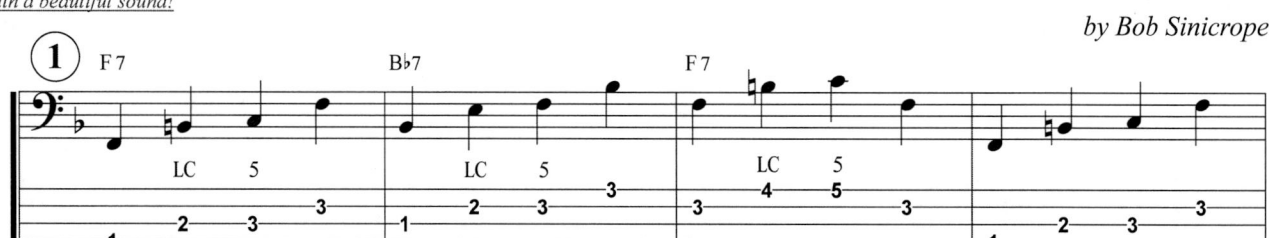

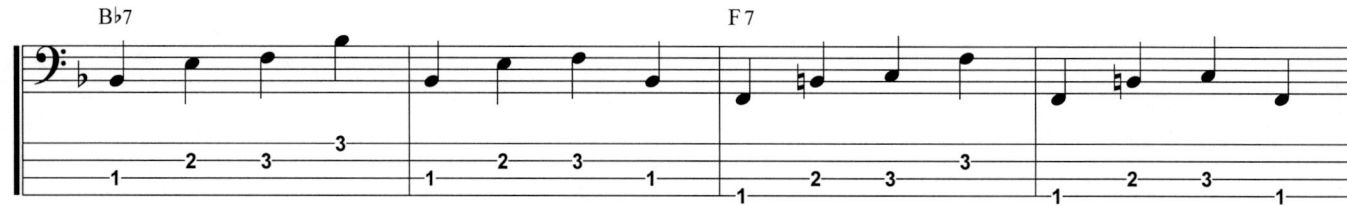

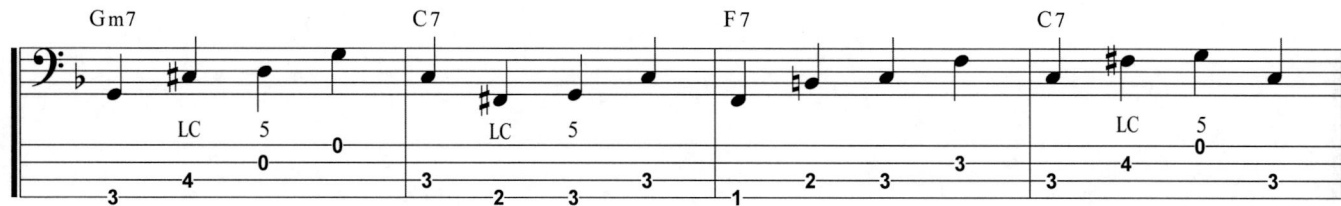

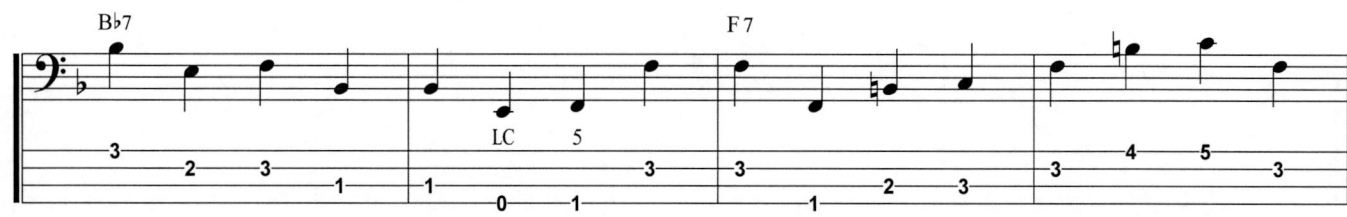

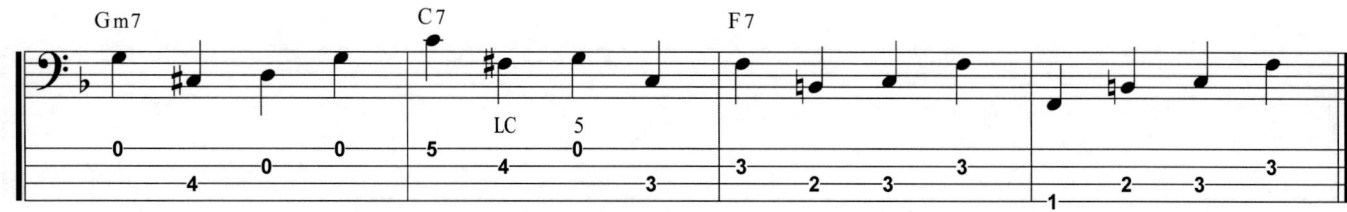

Inspiration, Education, Fun
©2020 SeekingSpirit

Approach Notes are tension notes that resolve to chord tones. They add melodic interest and create rhythmic motion. The resolution is stronger if the approach note is on an upbeat and the chord tone is on a downbeat.

This exercise features **Upper Scalar (US)** approach notes to the **5th (5)**. These work well in bass lines.

Connect with the backing track!

F Blues
Walking Bass Line
Add the 5th - Upper Scalar to 5th

To more fully internalize:
1. Listen
2. Sing
3. Play

by Bob Sinicrope

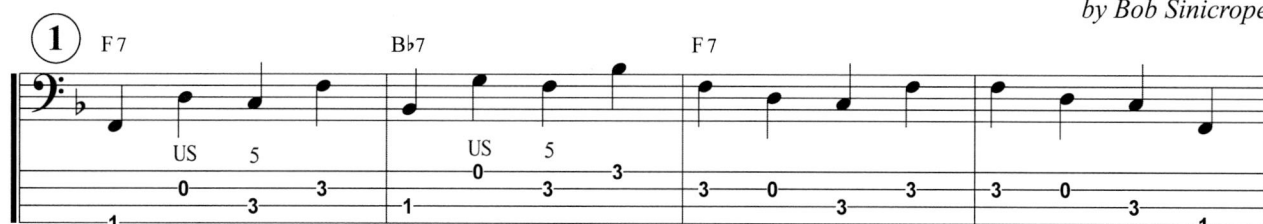

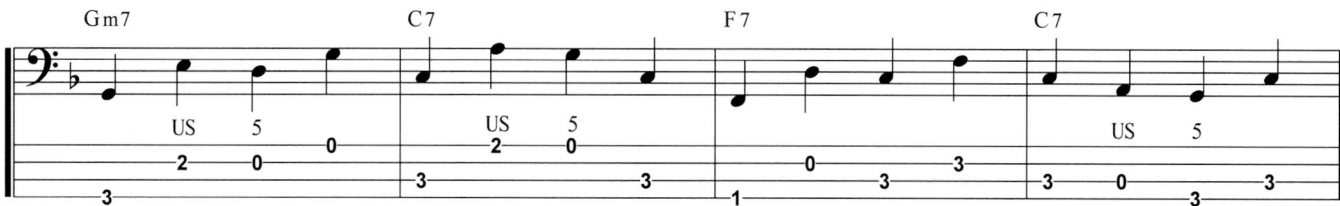

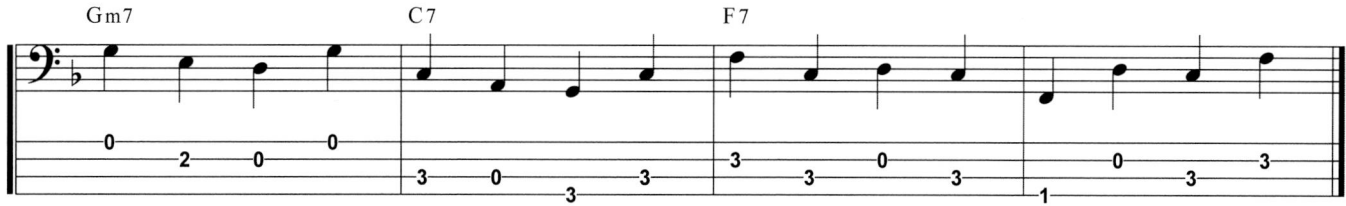

Inspiration, Education, Fun
©2020 SeekingSpirit

Enclosures combine Lower and Upper Approach Notes that resolve to chord tones. They add melodic interest and create rhythmic motion.

This exercise features Lower Chromatic (LC) and Upper Scalar (US) approach notes to the 5th.

Focus on what you play!

F Blues
Walking Bass Line
Add the 5th - Enclosure

To more fully internalize:
1. Listen
2. Sing
3. Play

by Bob Sinicrope

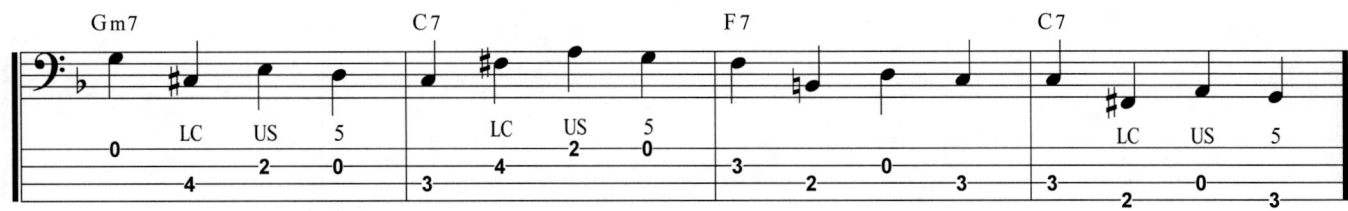

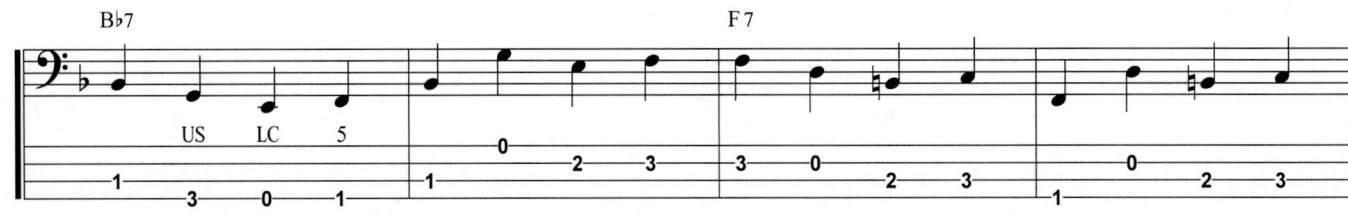
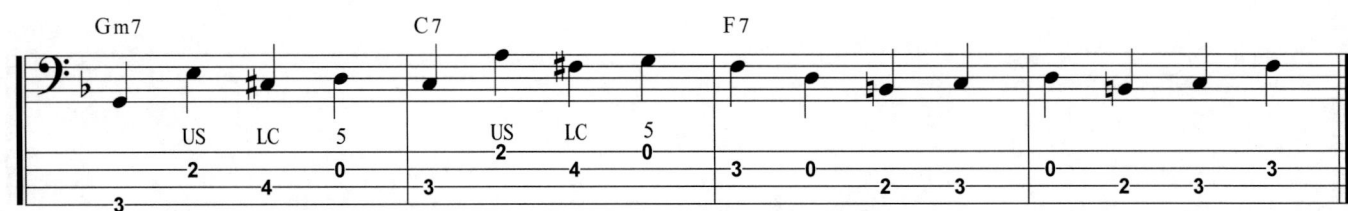

Inspiration, Education, Fun
©2020 SeekingSpirit

***Enclosures combine Lower and Upper Approach Notes** that resolve to chord tones*

Focus on what you play!

F Blues
Walking Bass Line
Add the 5th - Summary

To more fully internalize:
1. *Listen*
2. *Sing*
3. *Play*

by Bob Sinicrope

Inspiration, Education, Fun
©2020 SeekingSpirit

CHAPTER 3

Add the 3rd - Internalizing Root & 3rds

F Blues
Walking Bass Line
Add the 3rd - Internalizing Root & 3rds

Roots (R), Octaves (R̂) & 3rds (3) are the chord tones. The 3rd is a **Defining Tone** that determines if the triad is major or minor. Strong bass lines imply the harmony and defining tones strongly suggest the harmony.

Experiment creating your own bass lines with Roots, Octaves and 3rds.

Play with positivity!

To more fully internalize:
1. Listen
2. Sing
3. Play

by Bob Sinicrope

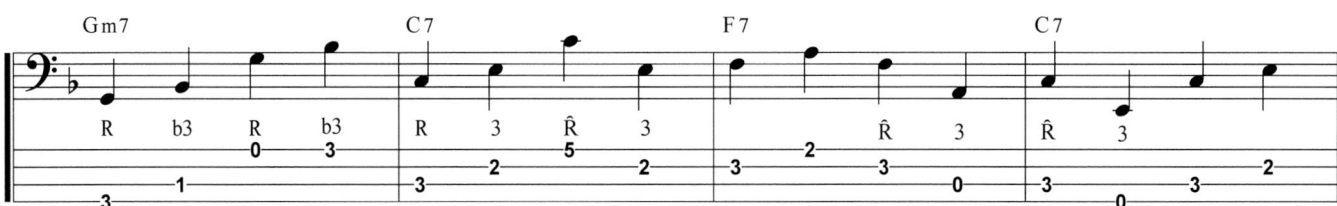
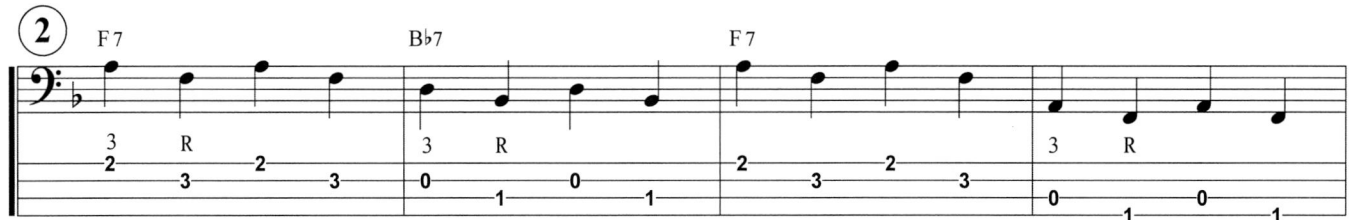

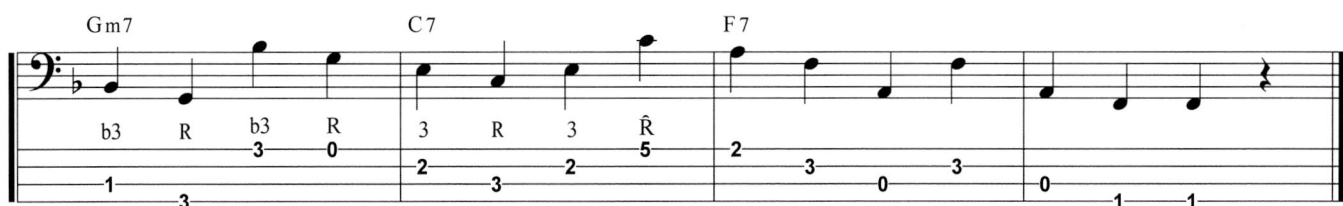

Inspiration, Education, Fun
©2020 SeekingSpirit

Roots (R or R̂), 3rds (3) and 5ths (5) are the chord tones of triads. Strong bass lines imply the harmony. Chord tones are the most powerful tones to spell out the harmony.

Experiment with your own bass lines with Roots, 3rds and 5ths.

Strive to play without effort!

F Blues
Walking Bass Line
Add the 3rd - Internalizing Triads

To more fully internalize:
1. Listen
2. Sing
3. Play

by Bob Sinicrope

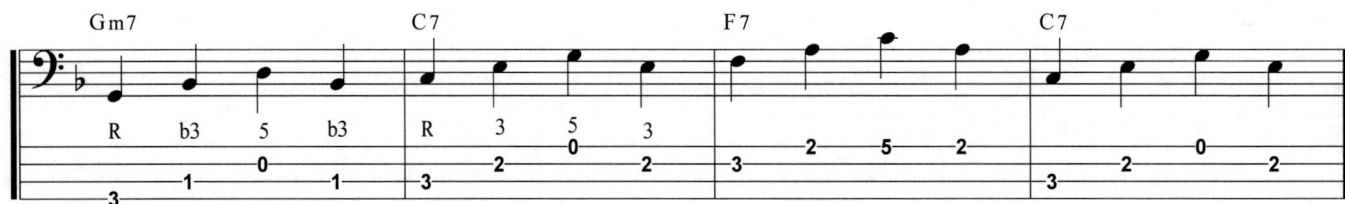

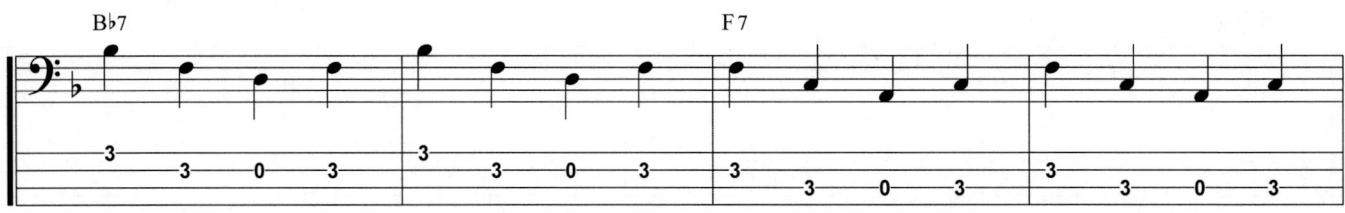
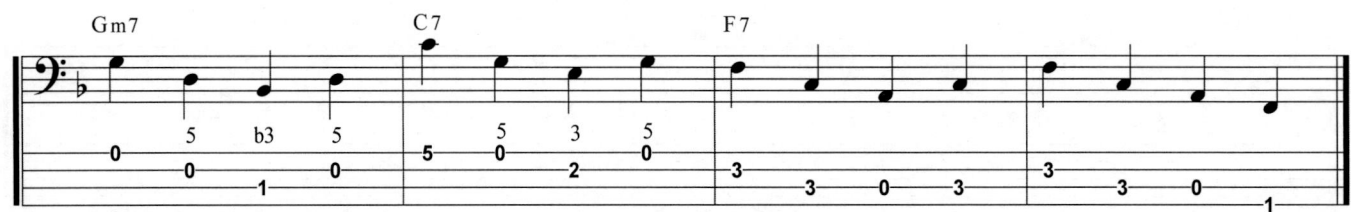

Inspiration, Education, Fun
©2020 SeekingSpirit

Approach Notes are tension notes that resolve to chord tones. They add melodic interest and create rhythmic motion.

This exercise features **Lower Chromatic (LC)** *approach notes to the* **3rd (3)**. *These work well in bass lines.*

Be the heartbeat!

F Blues
Walking Bass Line
Add the 3rd - Lower Chromatic to the 3rd

To more fully internalize:
1. Listen
2. Sing
3. Play

by Bob Sinicrope

Inspiration, Education, Fun
©2020 SeekingSpirit

WALKING BASS LINE CONSTRUCTION | F BLUES

This exercise incorporates the concepts presented in this chapter. Have fun creating your own bass lines that use Roots, 3rds, Octaves, Lower Chromatics, Upper Scalars and Enclosures.

Have a positive attitude!

F Blues
Walking Bass Line
Add the 3rd - Summary

To more fully internalize:
1. *Listen*
2. *Sing*
3. *Play*

by Bob Sinicrope

Inspiration, Education, Fun
©2020 SeekingSpirit

WALKING BASS LINE CONSTRUCTION | F BLUES

CHAPTER 4

Add the 7th - Internalizing Seventh Chords

Roots (R), 3rds (3), 5ths (5) 7ths (7) and Octaves (R̂) are the chord tones of the major, minor, dominant, half-diminished and diminished seventh chords. Strong bass lines imply the harmony and these tones are the most powerful ones to spell out the harmony.

Express Yourself!

F Blues
Walking Bass Line
Add the 7th - Internalizing Seventh Chords

To more fully internalize:
1. Listen
2. Sing
3. Play

by Bob Sinicrope

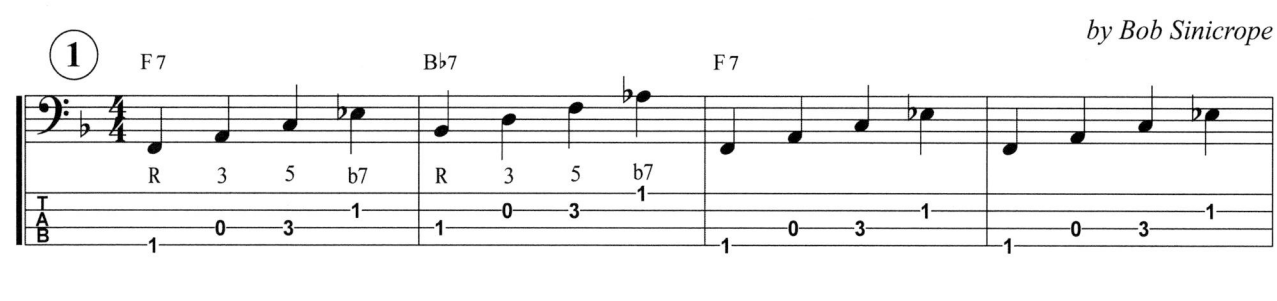
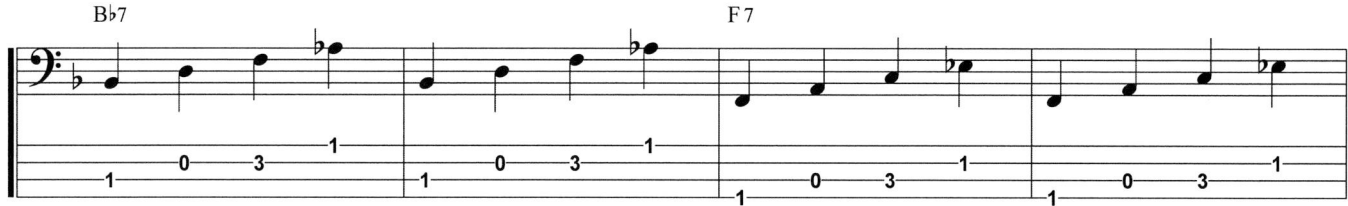
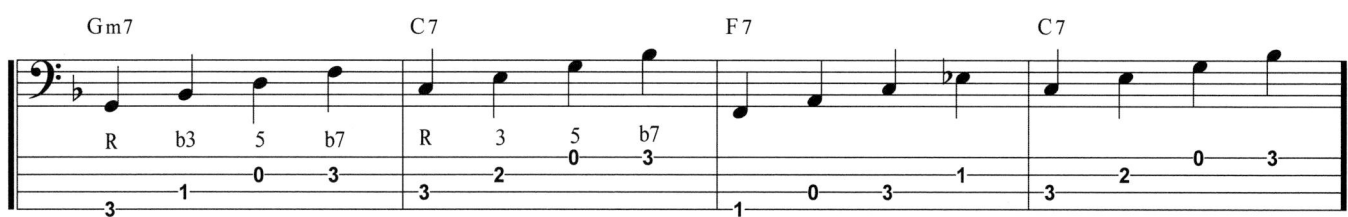
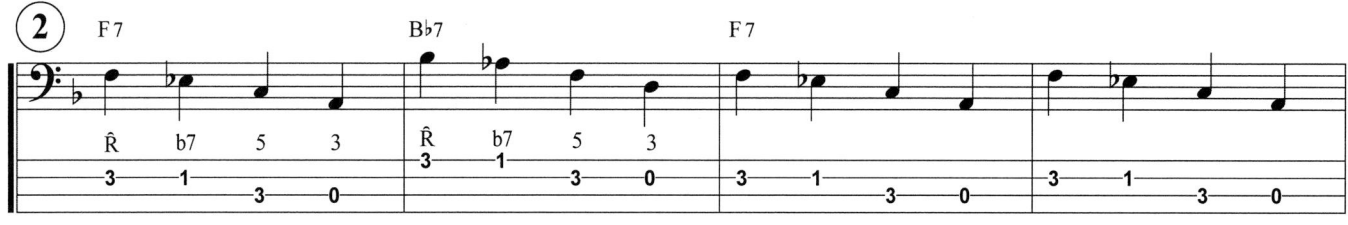
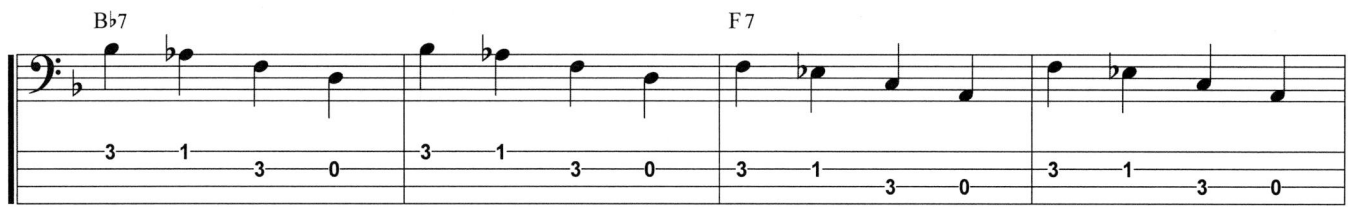
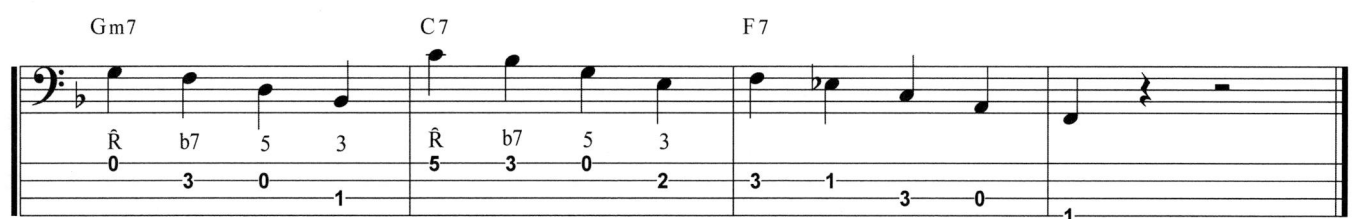

Inspiration, Education, Fun
©2020 SeekingSpirit

CHAPTER 5

One Measure Patterns

F Blues Walking Bass Line

One Measure Patterns - R235 532R

*A **Passing Tone** is a note between chord tones that connects them. The chord tones are consonant notes and the passing tone creates tension that resolves. Musical 'tension and release' is an important concept that adds interest and motion to your playing.*

Passing Tones make for strong bass lines.

Make it Groove!

To more fully internalize:
1. *Listen*
2. *Sing*
3. *Play*

by Bob Sinicrope

Inspiration, Education, Fun
©2020 SeekingSpirit

*A **Passing Tone** is a note between chord tones that connects them. The chord tones are consonant notes and the passing tone creates tension that resolves. Musical 'tension and release' is an important concept that adds interest and motion to your playing.*

Passing Tones make for strong bass lines!

Go for flow!

F Blues
Walking Bass Line
One Measure Patterns - Ř345 543Ř

To more fully internalize:
1. Listen
2. Sing
3. Play

by Bob Sinicrope

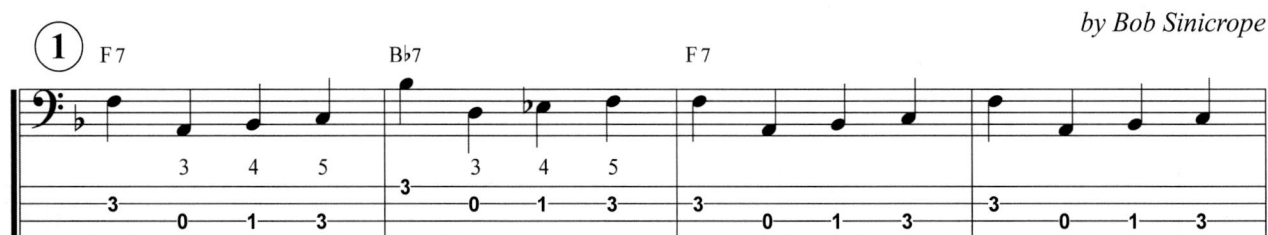

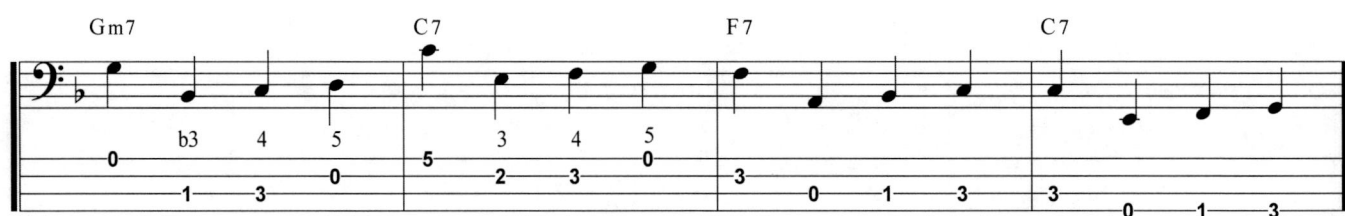

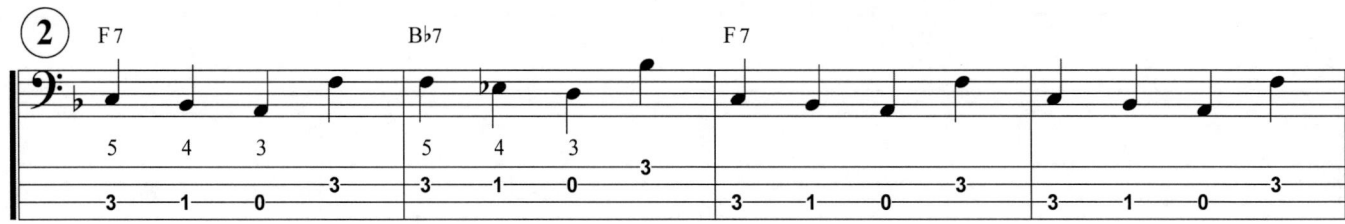

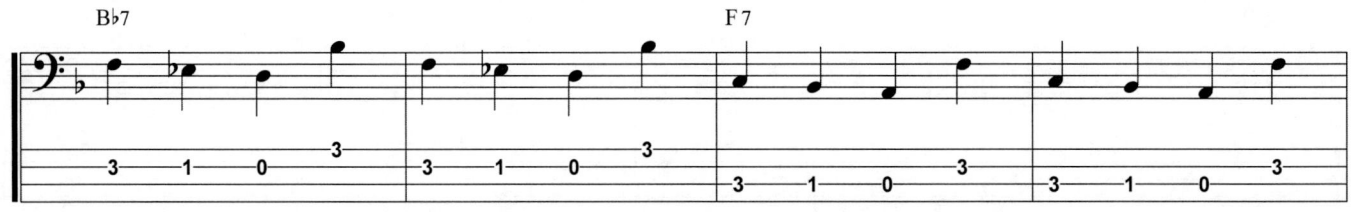

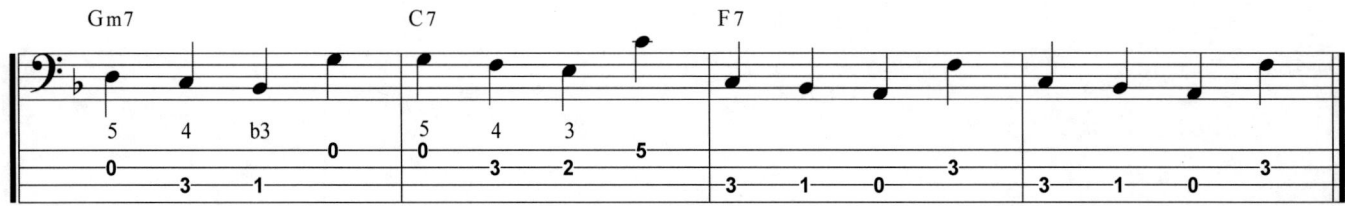

Inspiration, Education, Fun
©2020 SeekingSpirit

40 WALKING BASS LINE CONSTRUCTION | F BLUES

The 6th of a chord can usually replace or combine with the major 7th of a chord. The 6th is pretty but less powerful than the major 7th.

*This bass line uses a one measure pattern using the **Root (R), 3rd (3), 6th (6), 5th (5), and Octaves (R̂)**.*

Sing through your bass!

F Blues
Walking Bass Line
One Measure Patterns - R365-R̂653

To more fully internalize:
1. *Listen*
2. *Sing*
3. *Play*

by Bob Sinicrope

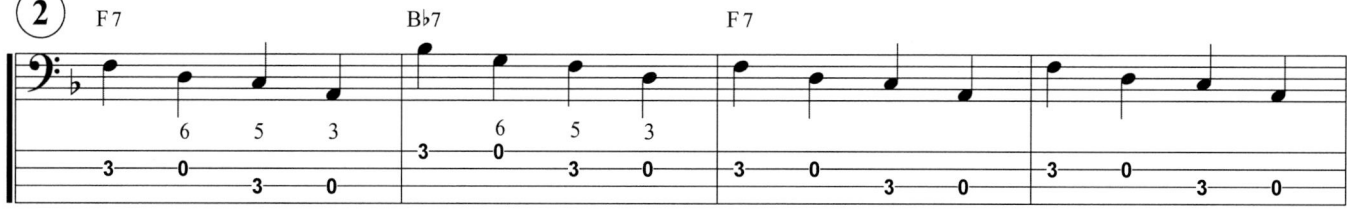

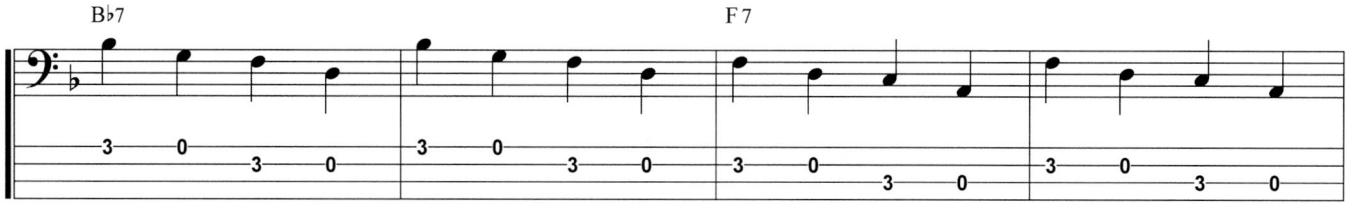

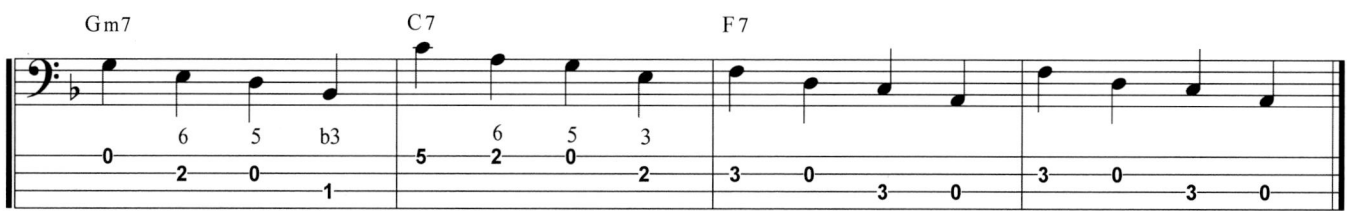

Inspiration, Education, Fun
©2020 SeekingSpirit

WALKING BASS LINE CONSTRUCTION | F BLUES

*These bass lines feature **Octaves (R̂), 7ths (7), 6ths (6), 5ths (5)** and **Lower Chromatic (LC)** patterns.*

Play as if no one can hear you!

F Blues
Walking Bass Line
One Measure Patterns - R̂765-R̂7(LC)5

To more fully internalize:
1. *Listen*
2. *Sing*
3. *Play*

by Bob Sinicrope

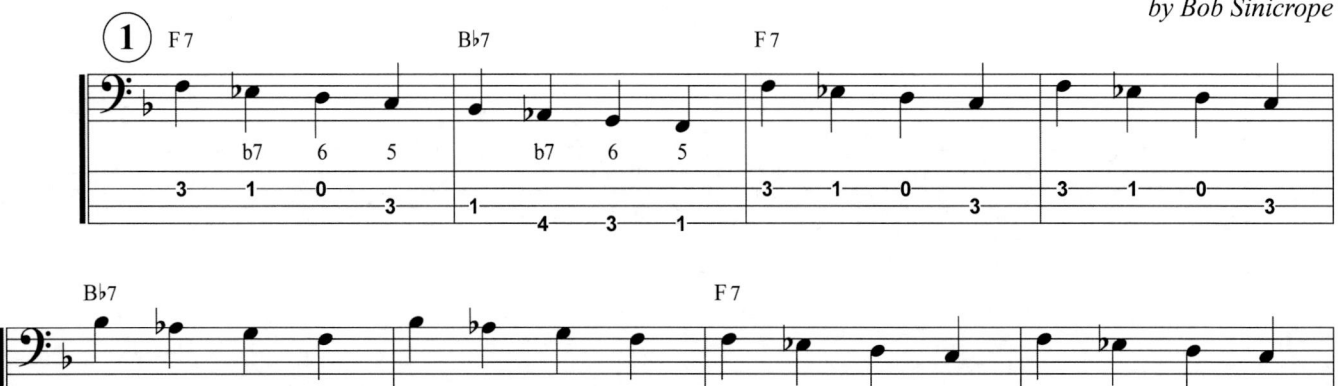

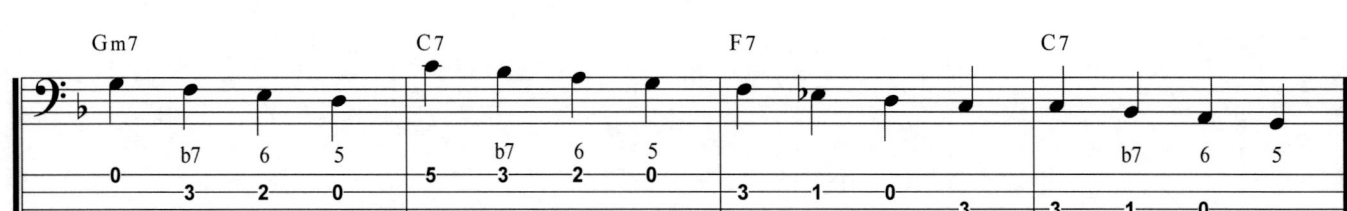

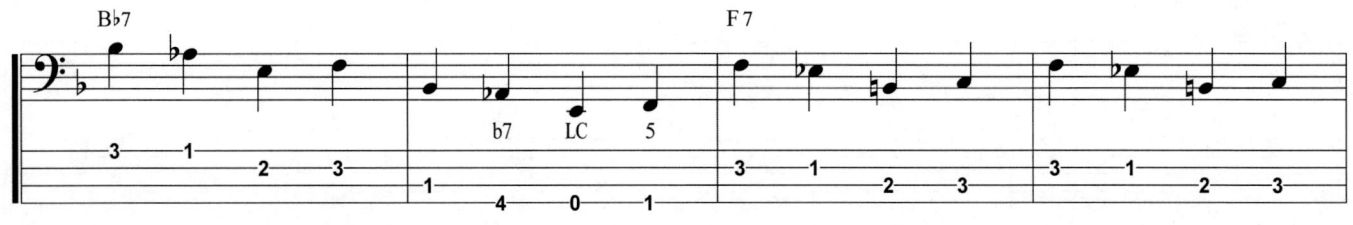

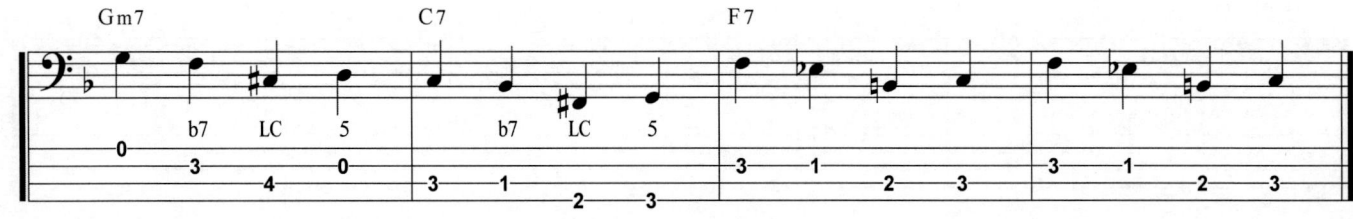

Inspiration, Education, Fun
©2020 SeekingSpirit

This exercise incorporates the concepts presented in this chapter. Have fun creating your own bass lines that use One Measure Patterns.

Strive for effortless mastery!

F Blues
Walking Bass Line
<u>One Measure Patterns - Summary</u>

To more fully internalize:
1. Listen
2. Sing
3. Play

by Bob Sinicrope

Inspiration, Education, Fun
©2020 SeekingSpirit

WALKING BASS LINE CONSTRUCTION | F BLUES

CHAPTER 6

More Patterns

F Blues
Walking Bass Line
More Patterns - #1

Passing Tones *connect chord tones. The chord tones are consonant notes and the passing tones create tension that resolves to chord tones. Musical "tension and release" is an important concept that adds interest and motion to your playing.*

Focus on how you can make the band sound its best!

To more fully internalize:
1. Listen
2. Sing
3. Play

by Bob Sinicrope

Inspiration, Education, Fun
©2020 SeekingSpirit

F Blues
Walking Bass Line
More Patterns - #2

Have fun creating bass lines that have patterns. This makes for melodic like bass lines that an interesting "shape" while still supplying accurate harmonic information.

Passing Tones *make for strong bass lines.*

Channel the music you internally hear through your bass!

To more fully internalize:
1. Listen
2. Sing
3. Play

by Bob Sinicrope

WALKING BASS LINE CONSTRUCTION | F BLUES

Inspiration, Education, Fun
©2020 SeekingSpirit

F Blues Walking Bass Line
More Patterns - #3

This exercise features scale like patterns. Scales are generally consisted of chord tones with passing tones between the chord tones.

Play as if no one is watching you!

To more fully internalize:
1. Listen
2. Sing
3. Play

by Bob Sinicrope

Inspiration, Education, Fun
©2020 SeekingSpirit

F Blues Walking Bass Line
More Patterns #4

This exercise features arpeggios of 7th chords and Voice Leading. Experiment creating "shapes" in your bass lines

Bring spirit, joy and conviction to your band mates!

To more fully internalize:
1. Listen
2. Sing
3. Play

by Bob Sinicrope

Inspiration, Education, Fun
©2020 SeekingSpirit

CHAPTER 7

Bass Lines in the style of . . . .

Pops Foster and Walter Page
Milt Hinton and Slam Stewart
Jimmie Blanton and Israel Crosby
George Duvivier and Oscar Pettiford
Percy Heath and Sam Jones
Ray Brown and Red Mitchell
Leroy Vinegar and Andy Simpkins
Paul Chambers and Ron Carter
Charlie Haden and Miroslav Vitous
Bass Line from Backing Track

These bass lines mimic the style of two pioneers of Jazz Bass playing, Pops Foster and Walter Page.

Learn about some awesome walking jazz bass players.

F Blues Walking Bass Line

Bass Lines in the style of
1. Pops Foster and 2. Walter Page

To more fully internalize:
1. Listen
2. Sing
3. Play

by Bob Sinicrope

52   WALKING BASS LINE CONSTRUCTION | F BLUES

These bass lines mimic the style of Milt Hinton and Slam Stewart.

Learn about some awesome walking jazz bass players.

F Blues
Walking Bass Line

Bass Lines in the style of
1. Milt Hinton and 2. Slam Stewart

To more fully internalize:
1. Listen
2. Sing
3. Play

in the style of Milt Hinton

Swing 8ths

by Bob Sinicrope

in the style of Slam Stewart

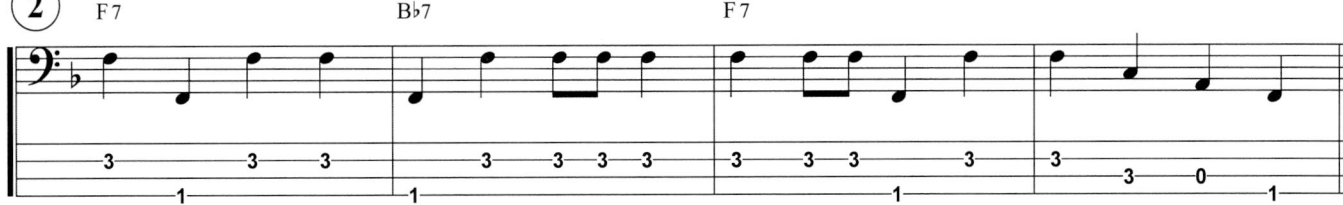

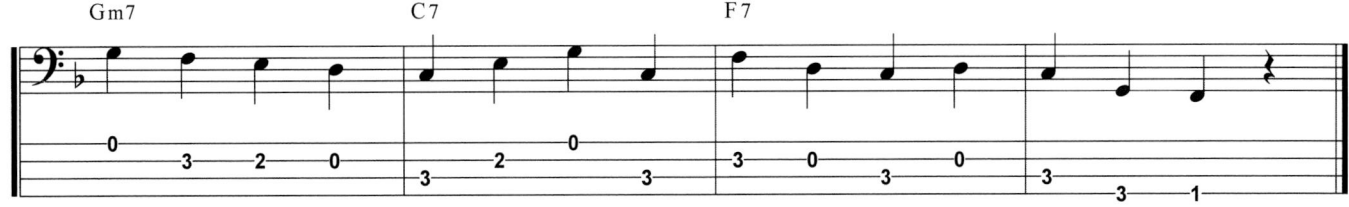

Inspiration, Education, Fun
©2020 SeekingSpirit

These bass lines mimic the style of Jimmie Blanton and Israel Crosby.

Learn about some awesome walking jazz bass players.

F Blues
Walking Bass Line
Bass Lines in the style of
1. Jimmie Blanton and 2. Israel Crosby

To more fully internalize:
1. Listen
2. Sing
3. Play

in the style of Jimmie Blanton

by Bob Sinicrope

in the style of Israel Crosby

Inspiration, Education, Fun
©2020 SeekingSpirit

54   WALKING BASS LINE CONSTRUCTION | F BLUES

These bass lines mimic the style of George Duvivier and Oscar Pettiford.

Learn about some awesome walking jazz bass players.

F Blues
Walking Bass Line

Bass Lines in the style of
1. George Duvivier and 2. Oscar Pettiford

To more fully internalize:
1. Listen
2. Sing
3. Play

by Bob Sinicrope

in the style of George Duvivier

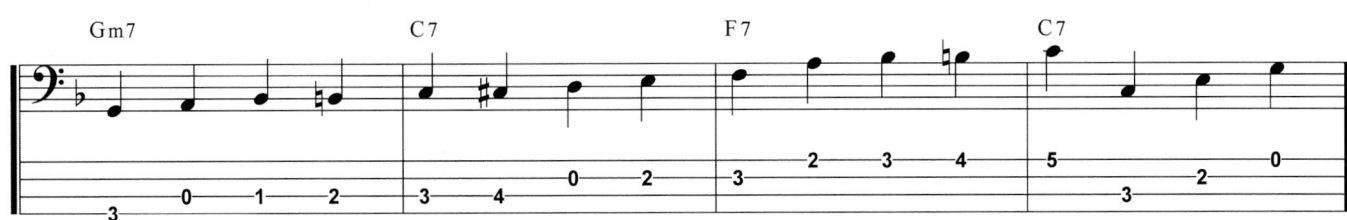

in the style of Oscar Pettiford

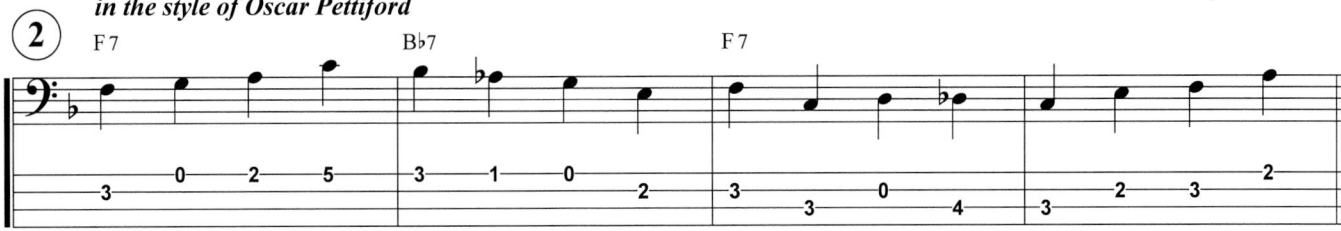

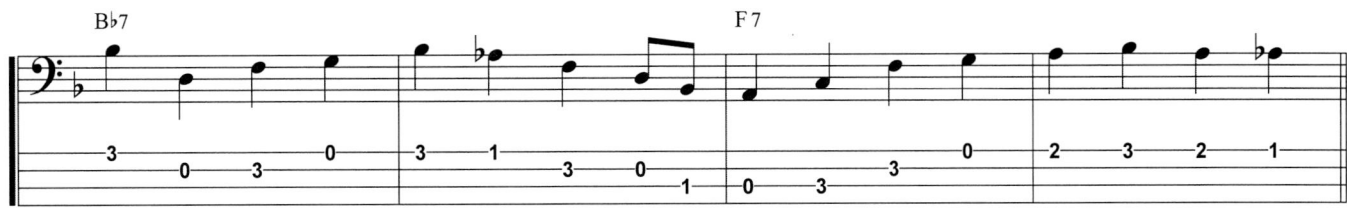

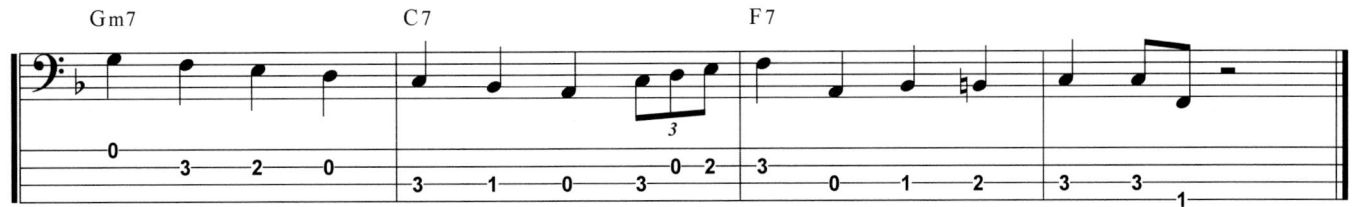

Inspiration, Education, Fun
©2020 SeekingSpirit

These bass lines mimic the style of Percy Heath and Sam Jones.

Learn about some awesome walking jazz bass players.

F Blues
Walking Bass Line

Bass Lines in the style of
1. Percy Heath and 2. Sam Jones

To more fully internalize:
1. Listen
2. Sing
3. Play

by Bob Sinicrope

in the style of Percy Heath

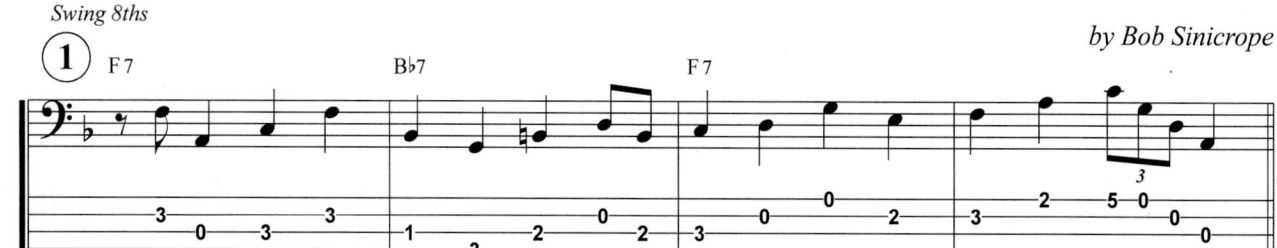

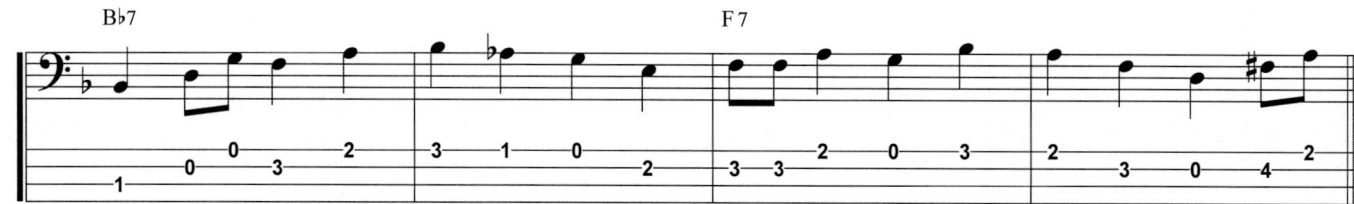

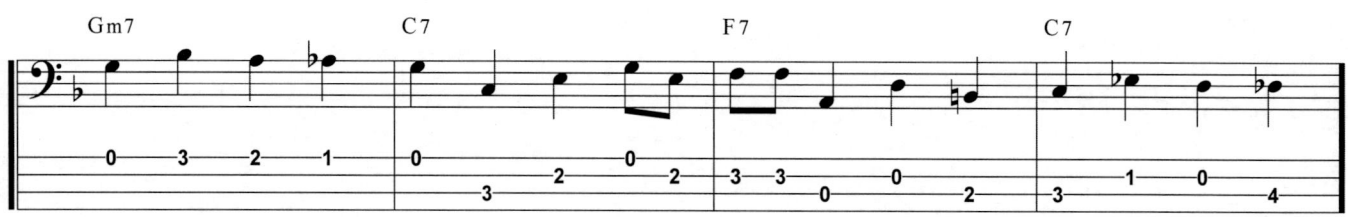

in the style of Sam Jones

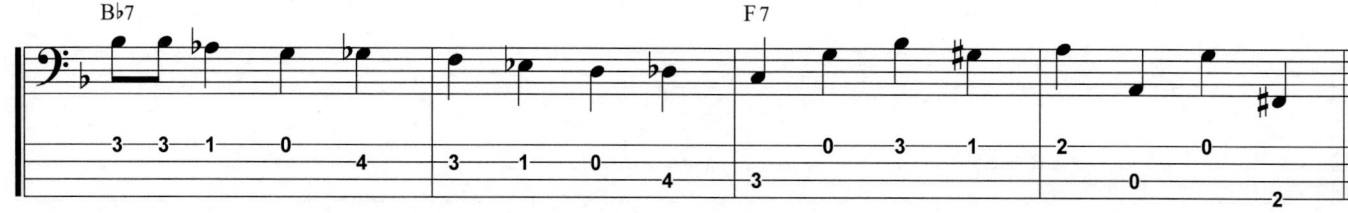

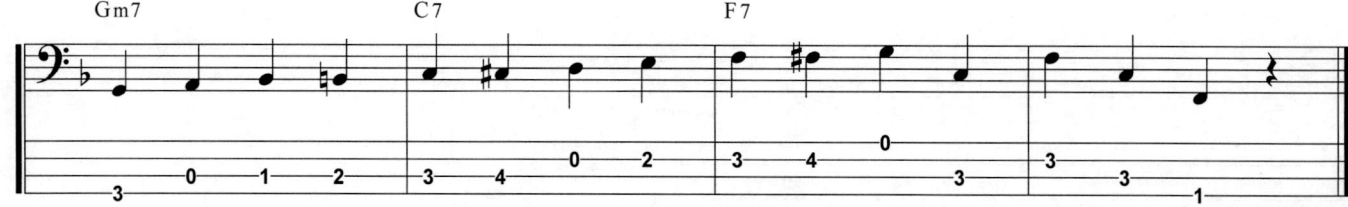

Inspiration, Education, Fun
©2020 SeekingSpirit

These bass lines mimic the style of bassist Ray Brown and Red Mitchell.

Learn about some awesome walking jazz bass players.

F Blues
Walking Bass Line

Bass Lines in the style of
1. Ray Brown and 2. Red Mitchell

To more fully internalize:
1. Listen
2. Sing
3. Play

by Bob Sinicrope

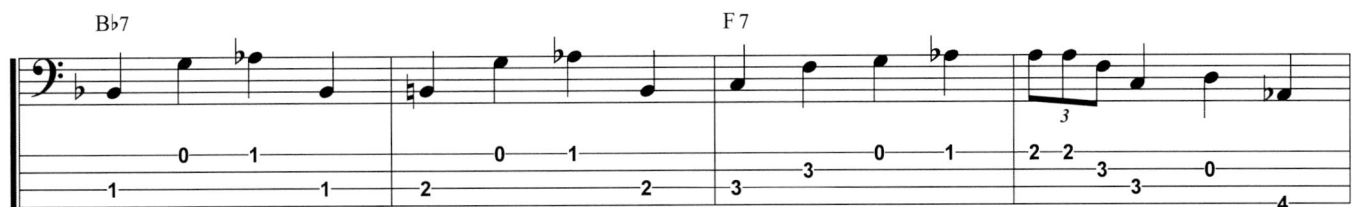

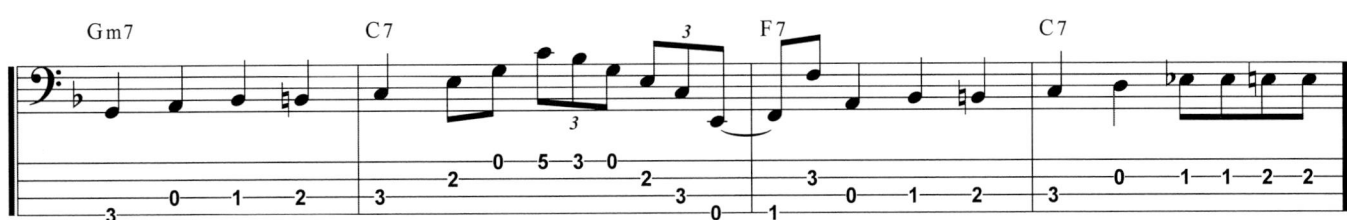

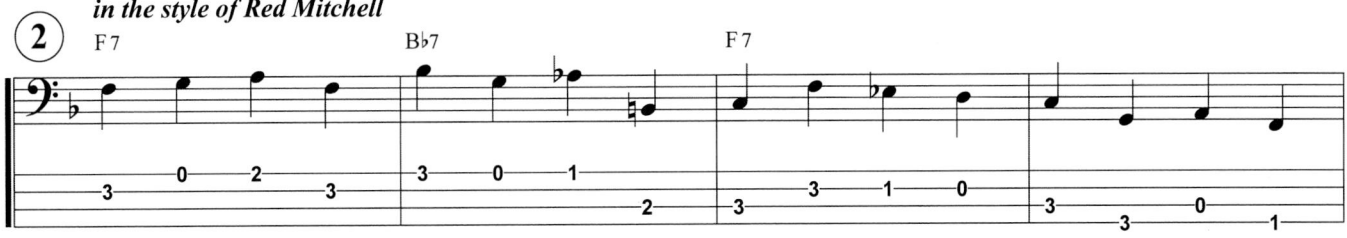

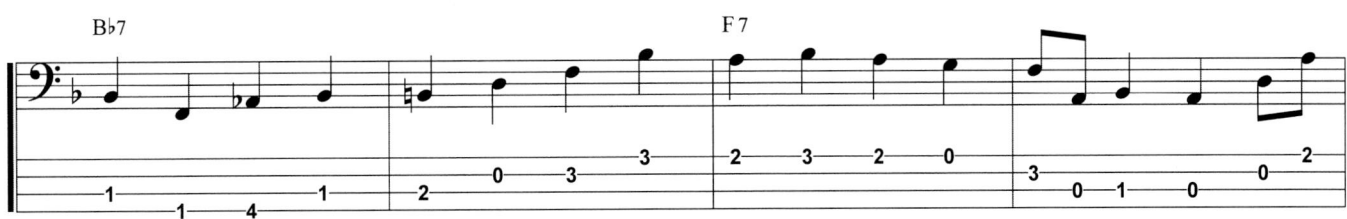

Inspiration, Education, Fun
©2020 SeekingSpirit

These bass lines mimic the style of Leroy Vinegar and Andy Simpkins.

Learn about some awesome walking jazz bass players.

F Blues
Walking Bass Line
Bass Lines in the style of
1. Leroy Vinegar and 2. Andy Simpkins

To more fully internalize:
1. Listen
2. Sing
3. Play

in the style of Leroy Vinegar

Swing 8ths

by Bob Sinicrope

in the style of Andy Simpkins

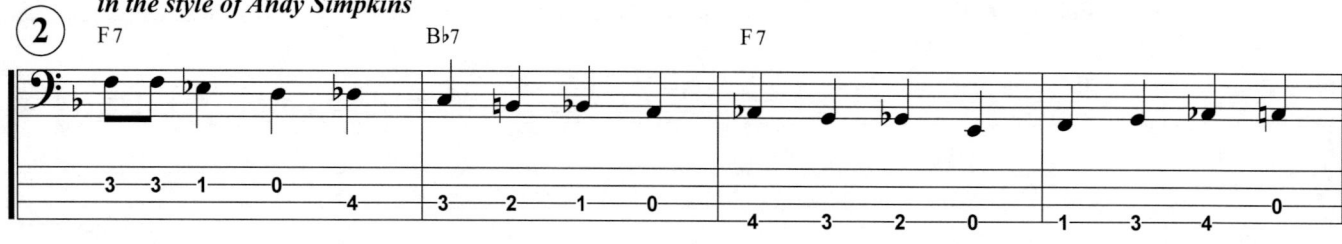

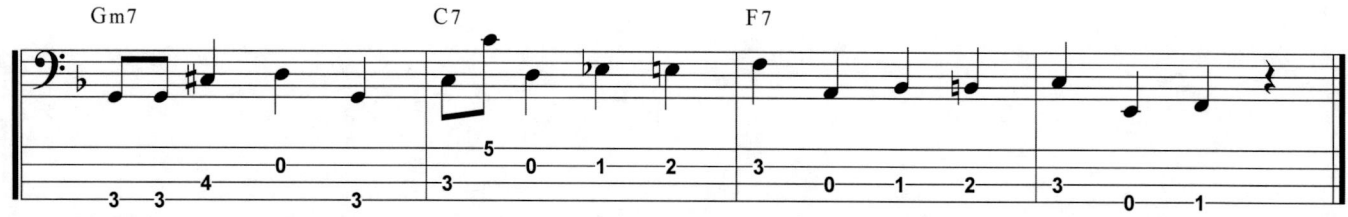

These bass lines mimic the style of bassist Paul Chambers and Ron Carter.

Learn about some awesome walking jazz bass players.

F Blues
Walking Bass Line
Bass Lines in the style of
1. Paul Chambers and 2. Ron Carter

To more fully internalize:
1. Listen
2. Sing
3. Play

in the style of Paul Chambers

by Bob Sinicrope

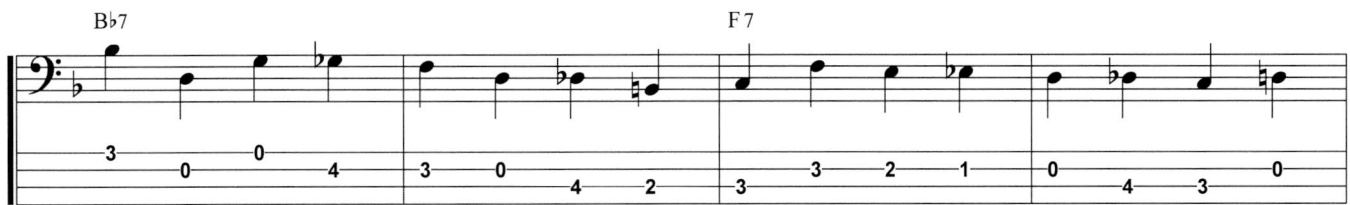

in the style of Ron Carter

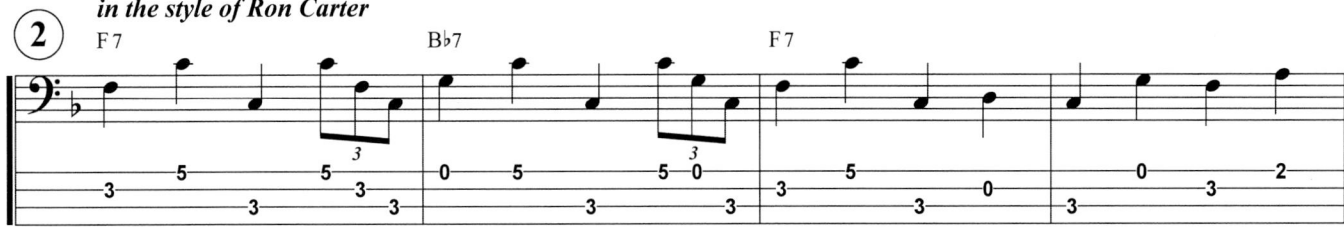

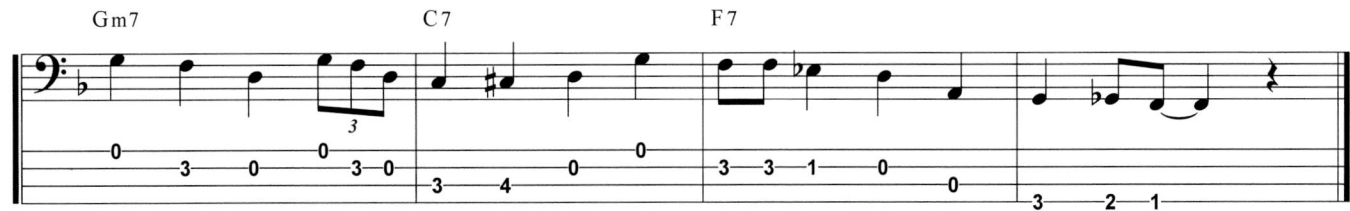

Inspiration, Education, Fun
©2020 SeekingSpirit

WALKING BASS LINE CONSTRUCTION | F BLUES

This is the backing track bass line.

Learn about some awesome walking jazz bass players.

F Blues
Walking Bass Line
Bass Line from backing track

To more fully internalize:
1. Listen
2. Sing
3. Play

by Bob Sinicrope

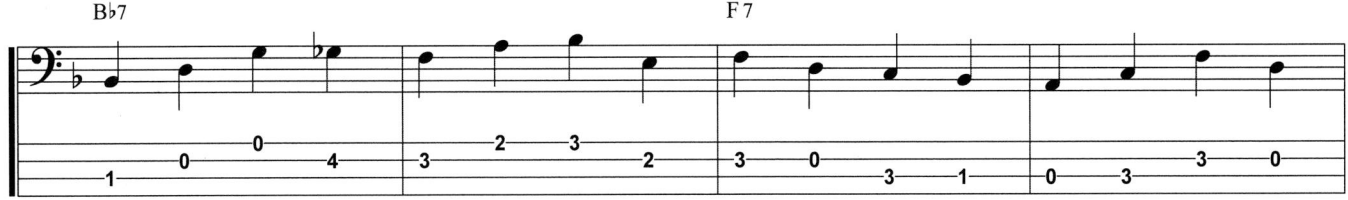

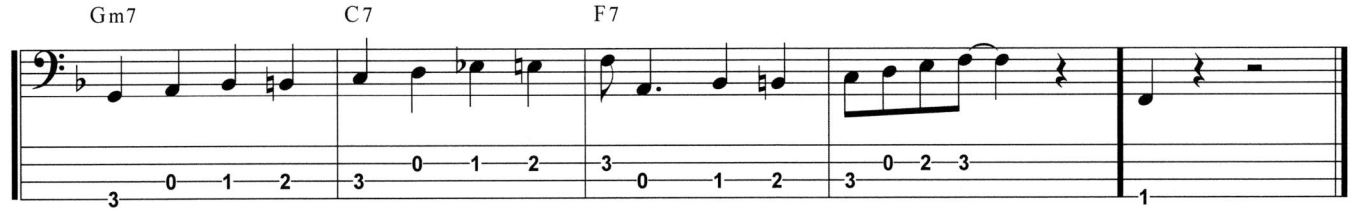

Inspiration, Education, Fun
©2020 SeekingSpirit

The Sher Music Co. Catalog

visit SherMusic.com for more information and to order online.

BEST-SELLING BOOKS BY MARK LEVINE
The Jazz Theory Book
The Jazz Piano Book
Jazz Piano Masterclass: The Drop 2 Book
How To Voice Standards at the Piano

THE WORLD'S BEST FAKE BOOKS
The New Real Book - Vol. 1 - C, Bb and Eb
The New Real Book - Vol. 2 - C, Bb and Eb
The New Real Book - Vol. 3 - C, Bb, Eb & Bass Clef

The Real Easy Book - Vol. 1 - C, Bb, Eb & Bass Clef
The Real Easy Book - Vol. 2 - C, Bb, Eb & Bass Clef
The Real Easy Book - Vol. 3 - C, Bb, Eb & Bass Clef
The Latin Real Easy Book - C, Bb, Eb & Bass Clef
Drum Supplement for Real Easy Book - Vol. 1

The Standards Real Book - C, Bb and Eb
The Latin Real Book - C, Bb and Eb
The Real Cool Book - Octet charts from the 1950s
The All-Jazz Real Book - with selected audio
The European Real Book - with selected audio
The Best of Sher Music Real Books - C, Bb & Eb
The World's Greatest Fake Book - C only
Jazz Arrangements of Public Domain Songs
The Yellowjackets Songbook - separate parts

LATIN MUSIC BOOKS
Contemporary Latin Jazz Guitar - by Neff Irizarry
Decoding Afro-Cuban Jazz - by Mauleon & Valdes
The Salsa Guidebook - by Rebeca Mauleõn
101 Montunos - by Rebeca Mauleõn
The Latin Bass Book - by Oscar Stagnaro & Chuck Sher
The Latin Real Book - C, Bb, & Eb
The True Cuban Bass - by Carlos del Puerto
The Brazilian Guitar Book - by Nelson Faria
Inside the Brazilian Rhythm Section - Faria/Korman
Conga Drummer's Guidebook - by Michael Spiro
Language of the Masters - by Michael Spiro
Introduction to the Conga Drum DVD - by M. Spiro
Afro-Caribbean Grooves for Drumset - JPhi Fanfant
Afro-Peruvian Percussion Ensemble - H. Morales
Flamenco Improvisation - Vol.1-3 by Enrique Vargas
Muy Caliente! - Afro-Cuban Book & Play-Aong audio
Music of the Arará Savalú Cabildo - Galvin & Spiro

DIGITAL FAKE BOOKS
The New Real Book - Vol.1 - C, Bb & Eb
The Digital Standards Songbook - individual songs with lyrics, plus C, Bb, Eb, High Voice & Low Voice
The Digital Real Book (650 songs from all our books)

THE DIGITAL SONGBOOK SERIES
The Kenny Barron Songbook
The Carla Bley Songbook
The Tom Harrell Songbook
The Oscar Hernandez Songbook
The Alan Pasqua Songbook
The Horace Silver Songbook
The Steve Swallow Songbook
The Ralph Towner Songbook
The Wayne Wallace Songbook
The Kenner Werner Songbook
The Randy Brecker Songbook
The Larry Dunlap Songbook
The Barry Finnerty Songbook
The Benny Golson Songbook
The Steve Khan Songbook
The Doug Morton Songbook
The Andy Narell Songbook
The Enrico Pieranunzi Songbook
The Dave Tull Songbook
The Denny Zeitlin Songbook

FOR STUDENT MUSICIANS
The Real Easy Book - Vol. 1 - C, Bb, Eb & Bass Clef
The Real Easy Book - Vol. 2 - C, Bb, Eb & Bass Clef
The Real Easy Book - Vol. 3 - C, Bb, Eb & Bass Clef
The Latin Real Easy Book - C, Bb, Eb & Bass Clef
Drum Supplement for Real Easy Book - Vol. 1
The Blues Scales - C, Bb, Eb, Bass Clef & Guitar
Rhythm First! - C, Bb, Eb & Bass Clef - by Tom Kamp
Guitarist's Introduction to Jazz - by Randy Vincent
Walking Bassics - by Ed Fuqua
Foundation Exercises for Bass - by Chuck Sher

CDs
Poetry+Jazz: A Magical Marriage - by Chuck Sher
Play-Along CDs for The New Real Book - Vol.1
The Latin Real Book Sampler CD

continued on next page

SHER MUSIC CO. JAZZ METHOD BOOKS
available in both print & digital forms

GUITAR
Jazz Guitar Voicings: The Drop 2 Book
  - Randy Vincent
Three-Note Voicings and Beyond - Randy Vincent
Line Games - Randy Vincent
Jazz Guitar Soloing: The Cellular Approach
  - Randy Vincent
The Guitarist's Introduction to Jazz - Randy Vincent
Contemporary Latin Jazz Guitar - Neff Irizarry

PIANO
The Jazz Piano Book - Mark Levine
Jazz Piano Masterclass: The Drop 2 Book - M. Levine
How To Voice Standards at the Piano - Mark Levine
An Approach to Comping - Vol. 1 - Jeb Patton
An Approach to Comping - Vol. 2 - Jeb Patton
Introduction to Jazz Piano: A Deep Dive - Jeb Patton
Playing for Singers - Mike Greensill
Wisdom of the Hand - Marius Nordal
The Jazz Solos of Chick Corea - Peter Sprague

SAXOPHONE
The Practice Notebooks of Michael Brecker
The Jazz Saxophone Book - Tim Armacost

VOiCE
The Digital Standards Songbook - individual songs with lyrics, plus C, Bb, Eb, High Voice & Low Voice
The Jazz Singer's Guidebook - David Berkman

DRUMS
Syncopation Companion - Bryan Bowman
Inner Drumming - George Marsh
Drum Supplement for Real Easy Book Vol.1 - Alan Hall
Afro-Caribbean Grooves for Drumset - JPhi Fanfant

TRUMPET
New Orleans Trumpet - Jim Thornton
Modern Etudes for Solo Trumpet - Cameron Pearce

BASS
The Improvisor's Bass Method - Chuck Sher
Concepts for Bass Soloing - Marc Johnson & C. Sher
Walking Bassics - Ed Fuqua
Foundation Exercises for Bass - Chuck Sher

JAZZ THEORY AND HARMONY
The Jazz Theory Book - Mark Levine
The Jazz Harmony Book - David Berkman
Forward Motion - Hal Galper
Metaphors for the Musician - Randy Halberstadt
Minor is Major! - Dan Greenblatt
Rhythm Changes Guide - Lukas Gabric
Jazz Scores and Analysis - Vol.1 - Richard Lawn
Jazz Scores and Analysis - Vol. 2 - Richard Lawn
The Blues Scales - C, Bb, Eb, Bass Clef & Guitar
  - Dan Greenblatt

PRACTICE GUIDES
The Practice Notebooks of Michael Brecker
Jazz Musician's Guide to Creative Practicing
  - David Berkman
The Serious Jazz Practice Book - Barry Finnerty
The Serious Jazz Book II - Barry Finnerty
Building Solo Lines from Cells - Randy Vincent

EAR TRAINING
The Real Easy Ear Training Book - Roberta Radley
Reading, Writing and Rhythmetic - Roberta Radley

RHYTHM SECTION GUIDES
Essential Grooves - Moretti, Stagnaro & Nicholl
Inside the Brazilian Rhythm Section - Nelson Faria
  & Cliff Korman
The Salsa Guidebook - Rebeca Mauleõn
Decoding Afro-Cuban Jazz - Mauleõn & Valdes

BILINGUAL OR LIBROS EN ESPANOL
101 Montunos - Rebeca Mauleõn
Muy Caliente! - Afro-Cuban Book & Play-Along
El Libro del Jazz Piano - Mark Levine
The Latin Real Book - C, Bb and Eb

MISCELLANEOUS
Method for Chromatic Harmonica - Max de Aloe
Jazz Songs for the Student Violinist
  - Kevin Mitchell & Joanne Keefe

Sign up for our monthly discount newsletter by writing shermuse@sonic.net